Hiccu

Written b
Illustra

Sam had hiccups.

'Hic!' went Sam,
and everybody laughed.

Rosie got a cup of water.
She said, 'I can stop your hiccups.'

Rosie drank a cup of water.
Sam drank a cup of water.

Rosie said, 'That stopped your hiccups.'

'Hic!' went Sam, and everybody laughed.
Mrs Hall said, 'Stop laughing, everybody.'
'Hic,' went Sam and **nobody** laughed.

Then Mo said,
'I can stop Sam's hiccups, Mrs Hall.'

She hid behind a door.

Then she jumped out and shouted, 'Boo!'
Sam jumped.

'That stopped your hiccups,' said Mo.
'Hic!' went Sam, and everybody laughed again.
'Stop laughing,' said Mrs Hall.

Tilak got a key.
He said, 'I can stop your hiccups, Sam.'

He put the key down Sam's back.
Sam jumped and Tilak laughed.
'That stopped your hiccups,' he said.

'Hic!' went Sam.

Then Mrs Hall said, 'Oh no!'

Loppylugs had gone.
Everybody looked for him.

Sam saw him in the playground.
Then he saw a dog.

Sam ran.

He shouted at the dog and the dog ran away.

Sam put Loppylugs back in his hutch.

Mrs Hall said,
'That stopped your hiccups, Sam.'

'Hic!' went Sam,
and everybody laughed.